E-Commerce

UNCOVERED

Mike Hobbs

E-Commerce Uncovered
This first edition published in 2003 by Trotman and Company Ltd
2 The Green, Richmond, Surrey TW9 1PL

© Trotman and Company Limited 2003

Editorial and Publishing Team

Author Mike Hobbs
Editorial Mina Patria, Editorial Director; Rachel Lockhart,
Commissioning Editor; Anya Wilson, Editor; Erin Milliken,
Editorial Assistant.
Production Ken Ruskin, Head of Pre-press and Production
Sales and Marketing Deborah Jones, Head of Sales and
Marketing
Managing Director Toby Trotman

Designed by XAB

British Library Cataloguing in Publication Data
A catalogue record for this book is available
from the British Library

ISBN 0 85660 899 8

Typeset by Palimpsest Book Production Limited,
Polmont, Stirlingshire

Printed and bound in Great Britain by
Creative Print & Design (Wales) Ltd

CONTENTS

ABOUT THE AUTHOR

Mike Hobbs is a freelance writer and journalist. His work has been published in many broadsheet newspapers and magazines, including the *Daily Telegraph*, the *Independent on Sunday* and *Time Out*. He has won awards for his corporate journalism and screenwriting.

Mike has written the **Real Life Guides** to **Plumbing**, **Construction** and the **Motor Industry** and **E-Commerce Uncovered**, all published by Trotman Publishing. He has worked for several organisations in the e-commerce sector and lives in London with his wife and their two children.

ACKNOWLEDGEMENTS

Many people helped me with useful thoughts for *E-Commerce Uncovered* but I would like especially to thank the following:

Adrian Gill
Jeremy Godfrey
Jessica Gould
Matt Hallett
Luke Heal
Andy Kudla
Phil Rigg
Sue Sillitoe
Kathleen Houston
Adele Cherreson
Dee Carey Pilgrim
Tim Dindjer
Mina Patria
Anya Wilson

And, of course I also thank my wife, Maureen, and our children, Anna and Jack, for coping with all the ups and downs of preparation and writing.

Mike Hobbs
August 2003

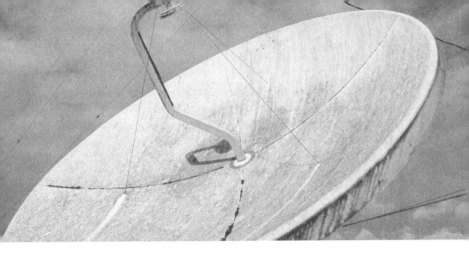

Introduction

There's been a lot of hype about e-commerce since it became a buzzword in the late 1990s. First it was the future, the way that all business was going to be conducted, and it was going to chase hidebound, traditional companies from their markets in the blink of an eye. Massive excitement was followed by equally massive investment.

Then came the dotcom crash, millennial in its timing and scything in its effect, and suddenly 20:20 hindsight kicked in. E-commerce companies were castles built on sand, doomed to impermanence. The industry was kaput. We – or at least a host of investors and business gurus – had all been deceived.

As often happens when perceptions alter so radically from one extreme to the other, the truth lies somewhere in between. E-commerce is not (yet) the universal answer, but it does have an important part to play in business. Crucially, it offers anyone entering it at a relatively early stage the chance to develop a stimulating and highly rewarding career.

So just what is e-commerce? A simple definition is that it is business conducted electronically, usually over the Internet. It is both narrower than Information Technology (because IT encompasses many jobs that are not directly related to e-commerce) and simultaneously broader (because many of the roles echo those in bricks and mortar companies and are classic sales, marketing, distribution and administration jobs). You don't have to be a technical wizard.

JARGON BUSTER

In the e-commerce world, a reference to a bricks and mortar company means a traditional one that sells its products to the public in an obvious, visible manner – through shops, stores, showrooms and warehouses.

For a pure e-commerce company none of these sales outlets exist, at least as far as the general public is concerned.

You may not be surprised to hear that a company which sells its goods through a combination of e-commerce and traditional methods is known as a clicks and mortar company.

However, while it is by no means essential to be an IT specialist to prosper in e-commerce, it's certainly no hindrance. And it is vital that anyone involved in the profession has a basic understanding of how things work in order to make properly informed business decisions. So there'll be a lot of IT talk.

This book is not an e-commerce primer, but it will give you a flavour of the different jobs in the industry to help you decide whether one of them is for you. You'll learn through case studies, typical working day examples, job rundowns and quotes so that you can put together a mental picture of life in an e-commerce organisation.

Your attitude and relevant skills will be tested by a series of quizzes, and you will be able to question your own values to see whether they match those involved in the industry. In short, you will gain every possible insight into e-commerce to determine whether it's the career for you.

For instance, descriptions of various terms that may be unknown to people outside e-commerce will be scattered throughout the book as Jargon Busters (you'll have just read an example). The point is to demystify the profession so you can make a clear judgement based on real facts, not through a smokescreen of unclear words and fuzzy images.

You will also be able to find out where you can go on training courses, pick up work experience or have the best chance to nail that elusive first job. If this book doesn't tell you precisely what you need to know on every aspect (and it's a bigger subject than any single book could possibly contain), then you will find links to websites and further information that will do so.

Who is this guide written for? If you're about to leave your school or college and are interested in finding out what e-commerce really holds in store, then this book is for you. You'll also find hints and suggestions about preparing CVs or PDPs (personal development plans) to present yourself in the best manner to potential employers.

Similarly, if you're stuck in a job that has no appeal for you and are considering changing your career before it becomes too late (not that it ever really has to be), then the book will prove highly useful.

But don't expect to become an e-commerce tycoon overnight. A new mood of realism now reigns, as some of the famous players involved, such as Martha Lane Fox of lastminute.com, will tell you. Like all business, it takes great ideas, great skills and much hard work to succeed.

Although you didn't need to be told that, did you?

DID YOU KNOW?
By the end of 2003 it is estimated that the total turnover for
business-to-business goods and services sold online in the
world will surpass $1.4 trillion (over 50% of which will be
spent in the US) – sound evidence that e-commerce is built
to last.

WHY IS E-COMMERCE SO VALUABLE TO US?

The Internet is not going to go away. As modern life becomes
busier and as security systems grow more advanced, barriers to
trusting in e-commerce transactions will be still further eroded.
What sells well on the Internet?

Typically, the goods and services that tend to shift fastest via e-
commerce are those that it is not necessary to see, touch or feel.
For instance, travel tickets or tickets for theatre shows, music
concerts, football matches or similar events can sell through very
quickly, particularly if the operator is selling them more cheaply
than via other methods. (Admittedly this is not always the case.)

Again, if goods such as books, tapes, DVDs, videos and CDs are
priced at a discount, then there will be many buyers willing to
purchase the large volumes necessary to make the venture viable.
Companies such as amazon.com, the usual success story quoted
in this area, rely on huge turnover to balance the very narrow
profit margins on each item.

By extension, the Internet is very useful for selling well-known
brands, where the customers know essentially what they are
buying.

At the other end of the scale, e-commerce can also sell rare or
niche brands very successfully, in cases where it is impossible for
the manufacturers to commit great sums to advertising,
promotion and distribution.

WHAT SORT OF PERSON WORKS IN E-COMMERCE?

So now you have a taste of the advantages that e-commerce can bring to consumers, but what sort of values do you need to have in order to be able to flourish in the industry? Some spring instantly to mind.

You must want to use your flair to provide a service with a difference. You must have honesty and integrity to build trust in your customers. You must be flexible, able to react quickly to events, yet not stray from following a clear strategic path. You must want to improve your offering constantly to stay ahead of the competition.

As well as these outward values, you need to have ingrained qualities to prosper in the industry. Most of these qualities are of course useful for success in any job.

Various people involved in e-commerce will soon be giving you their advice on what it takes to make your mark, but if there are four qualities that sum up the general required attitude, they are imagination, precision, thoroughness and an appetite for hard work.

There are other helpful qualities, so why not take this short quiz to see if you've got the right stuff?

QUIZ – WHAT ARE YOU LIKE?
What sort of qualities do you have? Are they likely to be useful if you choose to work in e-commerce? Answer the following questions as carefully and as honestly as you can, and the results should give you an indication about which jobs in the industry (if any) may be right for you.

Do you like to see the results of your work immediately?
TRUE/FALSE

Do you believe working with computers means less communication with other people?
TRUE/FALSE

Do you think customer service doesn't matter if you're not face to face?
TRUE/FALSE

Do you expect everyone to get all working details right first time?
TRUE/FALSE

Do you think teamwork is irrelevant in an e-commerce environment?
TRUE/FALSE

Do you find long projects unsatisfying?
TRUE/FALSE

Do you reckon that websites are not the place to express imagination?
TRUE/FALSE

If you have answered 'TRUE' to all of the above, there probably isn't likely to be a place for you in e-commerce or IT, unless you're a particularly brilliant techie.

If you have answered 'TRUE' to some or one of these questions, you probably need to examine what your expectations of the e-commerce world are, and make some rapid adjustments.

If you have answered 'FALSE' to all of the questions, you're already starting to think along the right lines to succeed in e-commerce. There might well be a place for you in one of the creative, marketing or administrative departments.

CHAPTER 1

Jobs in the industry

WHAT SORT OF JOBS ARE THERE IN E-COMMERCE?

What exactly is the range of work involved in e-commerce? Obviously there are a few likely roles you can start in, some requiring IT capability, others where it's not necessary, as well as those you can aspire to.

As we have seen, the e-commerce and IT industries are still capable of quite dramatic growth in some areas, particularly in services and the high-tech communications and software fields, mainly driven by expanding use of the Internet. In fact the rate of growth in the UK is being held back by the lack of availability of people with suitable skills. Despite the upgrading of recruitment approaches to tackle this problem, they have still been unable to meet demand.

For example, a recent report claimed that the supply of graduates qualifying from IT courses in the UK was way below the levels needed to fill all the existing and planned jobs. As a result there are significant job vacancies (around 10% of up to 1 million jobs in the IT and e-commerce sector), which is liable to make the UK less competitive in the global market. There is also a knock-on effect of wages and salaries rising to capture those who are available to fill so many positions.

In other words there are roughly 100,000 job vacancies in the e-commerce and IT sector. Although these, as already stated, tend to be at graduate level, there is no reason why, with some careful preparation and training, it might not be you making a case to do one of these jobs in the future.

Because information technology has completely changed the world in which we live. Ten years ago you wouldn't even have heard of the World Wide Web. Today, more than 72 million computers all over the globe are linked by the Internet. Almost all businesses rely on IT in some form and most engage in e-commerce of some description.

DID YOU KNOW?
40 years ago there were just six computers in the world.

Basically, it makes sound business sense. IT and e-commerce are used to reach more customers, to offer better services, to reduce costs, to improve efficiency. So a career in IT or e-commerce means you will develop highly valued technical and business skills, and you can work in almost any industry – from retail to healthcare, travel to financial services. You can also work in the public sector, such as in government or education. Crucially, your skills will be transferable.

More than 1 million people are employed as IT professionals in the UK today – 45% in the IT industry itself, and 55% working in other industries. The IT and e-commerce industries are still expanding rapidly, with IT Services (which often incorporates some e-commerce activities) growing at 38% in the last year alone.

Around 150,000 to 200,000 additional IT professionals are needed every year, and employers are recruiting from all sources – new graduates of all degree disciplines, school leavers, those returning from a career break, or those seeking to change career altogether, as well as people already experienced in the industry. As stated earlier, only somewhere between half and two-thirds of these jobs are being filled. This could well be where you come in.

Obviously there are many different types of job in e-commerce and IT, ranging from the business or people-oriented role through to the deeply technical. Most jobs however need a blend of technical, business and personal skills, the right mix depending on the particular position. Some examples of different jobs are included later in this chapter, to try to help you understand the range available.

Since new jobs are being created every day, you will not find every advertised title mentioned. Employers use different titles for similar jobs, so there are many titles not included here. However, you will find a range of typical roles to help you decide in what sort of area you are most interested.

E-COMMERCE AND IT SERVICES JOBS

If you're in e-commerce or IT Services, you are working for an IT company or a consultancy or agency specialising in IT solutions. Customers of your company will buy IT Services to help them implement, maintain or exploit IT systems:

- an insurance company might want you to design a new website;

- a gas company might want you to make sure their emergency call system is operational 24 hours a day;

- a travel company or airline might want you to design a secure online booking system;

- a hotel chain might want you to draw up a new IT strategy that exploits the Internet.

> **DID YOU KNOW?**
> Over 99% of all schools in the UK at both primary and secondary level are connected to the Internet. So, if you're still at school, why not use the resources at your disposal now?

You could be working either for a large global corporation or a small local business. You could work for an international consultancy or an Internet start-up. You could be involved in a range of activities such as:

- developing websites;

- designing and installing IT systems for customers;

- supporting customers who have software or hardware problems;

- managing projects.

The main thing to remember about jobs in e-commerce and IT Services is that you will be working for most of your time directly with customers. So you need to be skilled at working with people, enjoy being part of a team, be good at solving problems, and be able to keep a balanced business perspective.

Some examples of jobs in IT Services include:

- IT Consultant

- Project Manager

- Technical Architect

- Software Support Professional

- Hardware Engineer.

OPERATIONS JOBS

If you work in IT Operations, you will probably be working in the IT department of a company running the IT systems the company needs for its business. You could be working within retail or healthcare, travel or financial services – in fact, you could work in any industry, as almost all organisations today need IT. Yet again, you will see that the necessary skills are instantly transferable.

Quite often you will find that some IT departments also run the IT systems of customers who don't want to do it themselves.

Both of these activities are connected with e-commerce. You are likely to be involved in a range of tasks such as:

- helping people who are having trouble using the IT system;

- making sure the IT system is working properly;

- upgrading the system to add new functions;

- deciding how best to use IT to further your company's business.

As a rule, you will mostly be working with people within your own company, as part of a project team with your colleagues. You therefore need to enjoy problem solving and teamwork, as well as be able to develop the technical skills you will require. Such skills will need constant updating.

Here are a few examples of jobs in IT Operations:

- Applications Programmer

- Systems Analyst

- Network Manager

- Database Administrator.

SALES AND MARKETING JOBS

If you are going to work in IT Sales and Marketing, you will probably work for an e-commerce or IT company, promoting or selling its products, services and IT solutions. You will usually be assigned to a particular customer or group of customers, or you may specialise in a particular range of products or services your company offers.

For Sales and Marketing, the sorts of projects you could be involved in include:

- analyses of customers' business requirements;

- technical specification of e-commerce and IT solutions;

- managing a sales campaign;

- writing proposals to explain your recommendations;

- negotiation (with customers and internally).

In Sales and Marketing roles, you will be largely working directly with customers. You will have to learn about their businesses, and rapidly come to understand their requirements. You will then work with colleagues to come up with an e-commerce or IT solution that satisfies the customer's needs. You will definitely have excellent interpersonal skills, like working with others, and enjoy being in a dynamic, fast moving sales environment.

Some examples of jobs in IT Sales and Marketing include:

- Client Manager

- Technical Sales Specialist

- Marketing Professional.

RESEARCH AND DEVELOPMENT JOBS

If you work in IT Research and Development, you will most likely be employed in an IT company, creating new technologies or new products that your company can sell in the future. You could be researching new approaches to mobile communications, or developing a software game for teenagers or pre-teens.

You may be involved in activities such as:

- developing code for new software products;

- testing new features;

- correcting errors in software code before a product is made available;

- writing instructions for users of the product.

Research and Development jobs are very technical, and most also require good teamwork with colleagues. Some developers also work closely with customers because understanding what typical customers need helps the developer create successful products.

A few examples of jobs in Research and Development include:

- Software Developer

- Product Tester

- Technical Author.

MINI PROFILES

Here are some very brief descriptions of a few of the jobs mentioned already, together with others that crop up time and again across the various companies involved in the industry, placed in clusters to show what your chances of progressing towards them would be.

COMPUTER OPERATOR

You do exactly what it says on the tin. Every company involved in e-commerce needs to have someone who knows exactly how the network operates.

DATA INPUT CLERK

This is the most likely job you will get as your first in the industry. All companies will have loads of information that they need to update constantly and it will be your task to enter that data into the system.

DATABASE ADMINISTRATOR

As there is so much information to enter, it is more than probable that there will be several people doing it. It is also unfair to ask people new to the industry to be responsible for overseeing their own work, so an administrator with a guiding brief usually takes charge. This is a possible job for you on the promotion ladder.

ANALYST/PROGRAMMER (OR SOFTWARE DEVELOPER)

In this job you have to write the code that makes the computer programmes work flawlessly and efficiently. This is especially important in e-commerce where any malfunction in the system could cause huge losses in revenue. Again, if you show interest and aptitude, this is a possible job to aim for, but you'll need some qualifications first.

SYSTEMS ANALYST

Generally speaking, the next step up from being a Software Developer, where your task broadens to taking in whole new systems that need to be successfully computerised, such as the company payroll.

WEB DEVELOPER (OR WEBSITE DESIGNER)

If you show visual flair and a good feeling for design, then this is the job for you to express yourself. You will be responsible for the overall look of a new design or of a redesigned site, but you'll also need the technical ability proven by qualifications to undertake such projects.

ART DIRECTOR
Again, most companies have more than one Web Developer working on a project (or several projects) so there has to be someone who takes overall control of all the design elements. As in films, TV or advertising, that person is the Art Director. You'll aspire to this job if you have been a successful designer and have the ability to grasp the essentials of many projects simultaneously.

COPYWRITER
Every website needs words, and your function is to provide them if you're a copywriter. It has now been realised that this is a more specialist task than was formerly understood, so it is unlikely you could progress straight into the role, but it is a possible career development path if you show exceptional aptitude and skill.

PROJECT MANAGER
All e-commerce projects have many different elements within them and your job here is to juggle all these aspects to make sure that everything is happening on time, on budget and in the right order. This is not a position for the inexperienced, because it is certain you will be dealing with constant hassles and problems.

PRODUCER
This is an important job within any company, although definitions can range from a very senior role, where you are responsible for several projects coming to a successful conclusion, to a multimedia producer, where you ensure, say, the CD-ROM output meets all business and artistic guidelines.

ACCOUNT HANDLER
Although this position carries a lot of responsibility, because it actually involves keeping clients happy (no easy task), it is one that you might fairly target as a promotion, provided you show terrific communication skills, a quick grasp of e-commerce essentials and an unmatched capacity for hard work.

CLIENT SERVICES DIRECTOR
This job is one where you have to manage a team of account handlers and ensure that all clients are kept as contented as they can possibly be. Almost by definition, you will in all probability have worked as a successful account handler yourself.

CUSTOMER RELATIONSHIP MANAGER

It's quite an arduous task keeping customers sweet when you don't actually meet them, so don't expect this position to fall into your lap straight away. Again, you will usually have proven your drive and expertise as a customer relationship executive or account handler before taking on the role.

EDITORIAL DIRECTOR

Here you will be responsible for managing a team of copywriters and making sure that all the writing needs are fulfilled for all the company (or its clients). You also have to set the right standards and ensure that all your writers keep to them.

CREATIVE DIRECTOR

The buck stops here as far as design and words are concerned. Your job is to oversee the complete creative output of the company, ensuring it meets agreed standards as well as fulfilling the specific objectives laid down for each project.

NEW BUSINESS DIRECTOR

Someone has to ensure that there is a constant flood of new business into the company and, unsurprisingly, it's the requirement of this job holder. You would only be in the frame for this job after a very successful spell as an Account Handler (and maybe as a Client Services Director as well).

MANAGING DIRECTOR

Here you merely have to make sure that everyone is as switched on and productive as they can be, that clients or customers are equally delighted and that the profits are rolling in throughout. It's that simple. You could try it from scratch (by starting your own company) but I wouldn't advise it.

HOW COMPETITIVE IS THE JOB MARKET?

Although in general terms the industry does need more people, you will find, as in many other walks of life, that this does not necessarily translate into easy access to any particular job. In fact the competition for most places in the e-commerce world is pretty intense, although there is always room at the lower end of the scale for people just starting out.

Why is there this discrepancy between supposed supply and real demand?

Part of the reason is that there is now a ready market of relatively youthful people out there who perhaps took some time off when problems hit the industry two or so years ago. They are now queueing up to return to the e-commerce sector before their skills become too detached from the ever increasing technological advances. As a result, companies know there is a pool of expertise to draw from, with consequences for salary levels as well as competitiveness.

WHAT CAN YOU EXPECT TO BE PAID?

Your salary is obviously governed by many factors, such as the location and size of the company. London-based jobs, for instance, are likely to command higher salaries than those based elsewhere (but of course, this is usually more than offset by the higher cost of living in the Greater London area).

The following salary figures represent the range and average figure that you would be likely to receive for the jobs listed.

LEVEL	SALARY RANGE	AVERAGE
Director/Board level	£60,000–100,000	£75,000
Strategic Consultants	£45,000–65,000	£50,000
Interactive Account Director	£40,000–55,000	£45,000
(Marketing Services AD	£35,000–45,000	£40,000)
Account Manager (Client servicing)	£25,000–40,000	£33,000
Account Executive	£17,000–25,000	£22,000
Online Marketing Manager (Planning and buying experience)	£26,000–35,000	£30,000
Traffic Manager/Ad Manager	£20,000–30,000	£27,000
Project Manager (2/3 yrs' web management experience)	£26,000–45,000	£35,000
Assistant Project Manager	£22,000–26,000	£24,000
Senior Producer	£30,000–45,000	£38,000
Creative Director	£45,000–65,000	£55,000
Art Director	£35,000–42,000	£38,000
Senior Designer	£30,000–36,000	£35,000
Middleweight Designer	£24,000–30,000	£26,000
Junior Designer	£18,000–22,000	£20,000
Senior Developer	£35,000–£45,000	£40,000

Middleweight Developer	£25,000–£35,000	£30,000
Junior Developer	£20,000–£25,000	£23,000
Helpdesk	£17,000–£23,000	£20,000
1st Line Support	£20,000–£25,000	£23,000
2nd Line Support	£23,000–£27,000	£25,000
3rd Line Support	£27,000–£35,000	£30,000
Data Input Clerk	£11,000–£14,000	£12,000
Network Administrator	£30,000–£35,000	£32,000
Network Engineer	£33,000–£38,000	£35,000
IT Manager	£40,000–£60,000	£50,000
Head of IT	£60,000–£100,000	£75,000
Project Manager	£35,000–£55,000	£45,000
Business Analyst	£35,000–£45,000	£40,000

SOME TRENDS

The whole e-commerce market has become much more integrated with the parallel bricks and mortar world due mainly to three factors: the economic slow down, the worsening position after the dotcom bust and the consequent general call for more measurable marketing per £ spent.

Therefore e-commerce client services people who have survived in their roles in the digital marketing and integrated agencies have taken on online marketing and expanded their skill sets, running this alongside their project management skills rather than outsourcing this service as previously happened. In other words, they're doing more – but without getting salary increases.

Salaries for e-commerce client services in fact haven't really risen over the last two years. However, many of these salaries were a good £10K higher than those for their counterparts in the more traditional marketing agencies. So there has been some evening out of salaries and a resulting lowering of expectations from the e-commerce professionals since 2000/2001.

DID YOU KNOW?
48% of people in employment in the UK during 2002 claimed that using IT and consequently being able to engage in e-commerce was essential for their job. This figure has increased from 40% in 2000.

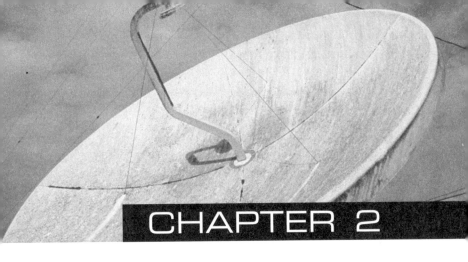

CHAPTER 2

Case studies – careers in e-commerce

This is the section where you learn what it's really like. People who are working in e-commerce in various jobs and have done so for different lengths of time tell you where they think business is going and just what you can expect at each stage of your career. They also tell you how they got their first job, what they like best (and least) about their work and let you know what people are looking for now.

CASE STUDY

Matt Hallett is a Copywriter at Zentropy Partners, one of the leading website development and e-commerce agencies in Central London.

How did you get your first job – and what was it?
My first proper job (I'd done lots of placements beforehand) was as a copywriter at the web agency Circle.com. I was taken on to work on the adidas UK account, primarily because I was a worthy

enough copywriter but also because I had considerable experience in running and the project was specifically for the running community.

I reached that position after lots and lots and lots of hard graft. I've walked the streets of 'Adland' countless times with portfolio in hand. I've written hundreds upon hundreds of letters. The particular job in question was the culmination of a good prospective book of work (basically a load of ads that I made up and a few ads that I rewrote) and a lot of patience.

I went for an interview for the Circle job in January of 1999, heard nothing until June and found myself walking into the Bristol offices as a fully paid up member of the industry in the middle of July.

What has helped you to progress?

There are three things that have been crucial to my progression in the industry. First you have to be good at what you do. It sounds a bit egotistic, I suppose, but if you've not got the talent initially then it can be difficult to develop it, especially when there are a hundred others desperate for your job.

However, talent only gets you through the door. The next most important thing is what will keep you in the job. You have to listen and learn to those more experienced than you. There's only so much you can do on your own and a mentor (be they a Senior Writer/Editor or Creative Director in my position, or anyone with experience in yours) is well worth finding.

Finally, I've found that a willingness to embrace diversity has been vital to my success. Particularly in agency environments, you're likely to be writing for a tech client one moment and a beauty client the next. The ability to jump from speaking to one target audience to another will keep your bosses from looking elsewhere.

Can you summarise a typical working day?

Working days are generally governed by the project you're required to work on. However, they usually follow a similar format.

I get into the office between 9 and 9.30am, check emails and get up to speed with requirements for the day. If I'm carrying on with a piece of work from the previous day then I'll get straight back into writing until lunchtime. If a new project needs starting then I'll usually have either a meeting or briefing session to run through the requirements, desired outcomes and timelines.

After lunch it usually turns out to be more of the same. Generally, specific projects would come to a close nearer the end of the day, which gives cause for discussions with Project Managers or Designers with regard to next steps, or conference calls with clients to review work and approve it where required.

Naturally there's also the odd game of pool, coffee break or the like intermingled with the day-to-day events, plus general meetings throughout the day on specific client development, brainstorms or pitch discussions.

What are the best things (and the worst) about your job?
The best thing about my job is seeing all the hard work come to fruition. I've only ever wanted to be a copywriter so it's quite a labour of love, and seeing my work on a website, in a newspaper or on TV is extremely satisfying.

The worst thing, probably, is having to remember that the client is always right. Your opinions, whilst valid, can often be shelved in favour of client demands. Ultimately the client pays your wages so it's a good idea not to disagree with their viewpoints too much – constructive criticism of a client is about as far as you should go. You have to learn to bite your lip sometimes.

Does the company generate its own social life after working hours?
There's no specific 'social life' outside of work but there's always a local pub to go to if the need arises. You generally find yourself working with a core team of people, so it's natural to then go out and let your hair down a bit after work.

Personally, I live quite a long way from the office so I always keep my socialising to a minimum. I try to cultivate the habit of getting home before 8.30pm.

Have you any advice for school leavers wishing to enter e-commerce?
Simple – develop the will to succeed. Want it more than the next person and don't stop until you've made it.

Can you identify any qualities that make people more likely to succeed?
I believe there are four vital attributes:

- competitiveness to want to get your important break in the first place;

- self-belief for the times that clients or projects become a burden or you get knocked back for the umpteenth time;

- creativity to be able to come to a project with a stream of ideas;

- desire to do the best work you can.

What do you think the future holds for you/the industry?
I'm at the stage in my career where I now have one of two possible routes to take. I can either step into the realm of the Creative Director or go it alone and work as a freelancer. I'm still undecided as to my chosen path.

As for the industry, I think it's now largely over the 'bump' of the dotcom crash. Companies are far more intelligent now and clients are starting to realise the full potential of this industry. I predict that the future of the industry will only improve, whilst other advertising media could see a downfall in demand.

CASE STUDY

Luke Heal is a Project Manager at Syzygy, a digital media agency and leading e-commerce provider in Central London.

How did you get your first job – and what was it?
I was taken on as a project coordinator – a kind of Junior Project Manager. I got the interview through a friend of a friend of a friend – though this was out of sheer luck it shows the

importance of networking and contacts. I think they gave me the job because I had experience working in the HR department of a large investment bank on complex data and knew standard office applications like Word and Excel. I had also been involved in IT, though this was not my main strength. I had also taken three months to research Internet production so I had a good general knowledge of the area, though no professional experience.

What has helped you to progress?
Generally, I've tried to cultivate an ability to talk to technical and design staff and understand the fundamentals of what they do, and then communicate this internally and to clients. I also have an eye for detail and thoroughness (much of project management is about checking people's work). And you always need determination to bounce back from difficult client or internal situations and learn from them. As project management is something you tend to learn the hard way, any mentoring you can get is valuable.

Can you summarise a typical working day?
Project managers spend much of their time planning other people's time as well as their own. I typically spend the morning reading all my emails and recording them in whatever issues lists I am using. I also check what human resources are assigned to the project(s) I am managing and make sure that they all know what they are doing and have everything they need to do their work. Having people sitting around doing nothing is to be avoided at all costs.

Prioritising what project or client issues should be responded to first is important as, though some clients or internal figures shout louder, their work may not need to happen first. I do have to take any calls when they come through, however! Once the work is planned I will work through each element of it as methodically as I can, either resolving current project issues or planning or selling in future work.

What are the best things (and the worst) about your job?
Project work of any kind is very delivery focused. The best times are immediately when a deadline is met, and the worst times – though exciting – are immediately before a deadline – especially if

you are running late. Though working hours are often long they are also flexible and if you are good at planning and managing your time you can do most things that you want to do. My job can be very varied – I work on all kinds of different projects – and this can be really interesting. I quite enjoy learning about new technologies, too.

Does the company generate its own social life after working hours?
Working in an agency is often very social. The attitude is often to have your cake and eat it too – in the sense that you are expected to produce professional work, but in a relaxed environment. The theory is that people do not produce their best work when stressed, or wearing an uncomfortable suit.

Have you any advice for school leavers wishing to enter e-commerce?
It is probably best to decide which aspect of e-commerce you wish to specialise in as early as possible. Increasingly, the Internet will not really be divisible from TV, mobile phones etc, so you need to decide if your heart lies in the technical, artistic, management or marketing sides – rather than in 'the Internet' per se. Ultimately, the Internet is just a particular kind of technology – while some kind of understanding of the logic behind the technology is important, your skills should be transferable across different media.

Can you identify any qualities that make people more likely to succeed?
The ability to listen and bring clarity with your communications is important. If you are working for a client you need to produce work that suits their needs, and if you are managing people you need to tell them what to do clearly. It helps if you can inspire people to do what you think is the best thing, too.

What do you think the future holds for you/the industry?
While the industry has taken some serious knocks in the last two years, the future of Internet-related technologies is assured. The Internet is already very much a part of modern life and becoming more, not less, important to many kinds of work. When the shockwaves from the 'dotcom' era have fully died away the

Internet will become just another medium – like TV or radio – and an important one at that. As for me personally, I am steadily adding to my experience with each different project. Hopefully, my skills are pretty transferable, so I may end up trying my hand at project-managing something outside of e-commerce, like a large construction project or movie production.

CASE STUDY

Jeremy Godfrey is a partner and director of In The House, a small agency in North London providing website development and e-commerce services.

How did you get your first job – and what was it?

After doing an Economics degree I found I didn't have the right set of skills to get the job in IT that I was after. I then completed a Masters in Information Systems Development. Again my practical skills were lacking but the MSc gave me the credibility to get a job in a small software house in the City as an implementation support analyst.

In reality, I was only the seventh person in the office (the company had its HQ in New York). As a result I wore a number of additional hats: pre-sales support, account manager, project manager, office secretary, office hardware support. I ended up a regular jack of all trades. It was a great learning experience.

What has helped you to progress?

The fact that in the early days I was dropped in at the deep end – I had to sink or swim. In the two years I was in this job I learned more than I should have done because I had to. Variety is not only the spice of life but you'll also find it is often the key to progression. These skills gave me the confidence to start up an Internet company.

Unfortunately, it was a case of 'right idea, wrong time' (this was early 2000 when the Internet bubble was bursting) and as soon as that had gone to the wall I had to look around. In no time at all I'd been hired as a consultant to project-manage the development of a broadband business portal for Telewest Blueyonder. Once this contract had expired I realised, perhaps too confidently, I could do it better myself and so I got together with a like-minded friend and, shortly afterwards, In The House was born.

Can you summarise a typical working day?

I always struggle to get out of bed in the morning, but fortunately it's a short journey to work. It's also very easy to park, which is another bonus.

The first thing I do is go through my emails. This usually includes a whole pile of newsletters so I'm able to catch up on industry news.

There's often the risk that I have to fix some sort of office hardware technical issue. This can take up a huge swathe of the day.

Mid-morning I have a daily update meeting with my partner and other members of company management. There are always issues and progress reports that need to be discussed.

Then, when I've finished the general routine, I try and knock off some tasks in my task list. Before lunchtime, for instance, I usually make some marketing phone calls – either following up warm leads or making courtesy calls in an account management role.

I find the afternoon is usually taken up with client meetings and preparation for client meetings. We try to schedule things this way around.

What are the best things (and the worst) about your job?

The best things are the variety, getting to research industries that I know nothing about, working in a very quick-changing environment, and the fact I don't have to wear a suit.

Conversely, the worst things are the large amount of competition, the fact that computers are annoyingly out of date (and if they're not, they soon become so), and the drip-feed from constantly demanding clients – although we need them, of course.

Does the company generate its own social life after working hours?
It does. We take an active role in sorting this out: whether it means going down the pub, taking a trip to the cinema or blasting away on the golf driving range. It is also important to keep up the socialising during working hours so that the atmosphere does not get too stale, generally by having a group lunch in the park in the summer, or perhaps having online gaming competitions at lunchtime.

Have you any advice for school leavers wishing to enter e-commerce?
The best tip I can pass on is to have a wide variety of skills. The core skills for the job are imperative, but what you need is to find something that will make you stand out from the crowd. Give yourself skills that are related to your industry but not directly relevant to your job, e.g. project management, time management.

Be eager – look for extra things to do. Try and get some freelance work for very reduced rates or for nothing (remember, it is a risk for the employer to use you). Make yourself an online CV to go with your current one. If you haven't got a good CV yet, prepare one. Get very directly related practical skills so that you can hit the floor running when you get a job.

Can you identify any qualities that make people more likely to succeed?
Are you a geek or can you be taken to client meetings? You need to be presentable. Do you have the nous to learn skills to do someone else's job if they're on holiday? Become proactive – show that hiring you adds value. Communication skills are vital for someone in development – you cannot lock yourself away in a dark room, you must make yourself an integral part of a team.

What do you think the future holds for you/the industry?
I must continuously evolve my skills and knowledge to at least keep up with the industry, whilst always looking to get one step ahead. The industry is very depressed at the moment as IT spend is down, so riding out the storm will prove very interesting and profitable when the upturn comes around. The market will also

inevitably consolidate, so partnering with the correct people and companies will prove crucial.

CASE STUDY

Phil Rigg is Editorial Director of Zentropy Partners, one of the leading website development and e-commerce agencies in Central London.

How did you get your first job – and what was it?

My first job was teaching literature at Uludag University in Bursa, Turkey. I'd just completed an MA in literature and philosophy in the UK, and my ex-tutor gave my name to a contact who was recruiting for this overseas teaching position. I worked in Turkey for two years.

My first e-commerce work arrived while I was working for a specialist writing consultancy in West London. I'd got this job by sending in a plain English translation of a technical medical text, with a covering letter saying 'Can I be of any help to you?' We supplied writing services to a large design agency that developed websites, so I was soon writing online copy for clients such as Lloyds TSB, Visa International, Royal Mail, Shell and Mercedes-Benz.

What has helped you to progress?

An interest in language has been my main springboard, manifested in four ways:

- My qualifications were all language based.

- I learned bits and pieces of foreign languages at school and after.

- I've always liked reading and ideas.

- I've always done my own writing – songs, poems, fiction, letters etc.

Long before I got a proper job, I knew hundreds of songs, poems, advertising jingles and other language snippets by heart. I still can't read anything without noticing its features or thinking how it could be better.

While my language background remains useful, I've had to learn a lot about IT to do my current job. Luckily I work closely with technology specialists, so I can always ask when I don't understand what's going on. In fact there's often a useful tension between the techie's expertise and an editor's plain English approach.

Can you summarise a typical working day?
A typical day might start with meeting the production manager and project managers, discussing what jobs we need to do and deciding who'll do what. The production manager is responsible for resourcing – allocating people to projects – while the project managers are responsible for steering the projects from start to finish.

Our work is varied – writing online banner ads, editing a client's web pages, creating guidelines for online copy, or checking our own colleagues' documents for clarity and accuracy. A single job sometimes stretches over several days – or we might find ourselves completing several jobs in one day.

I spend too much time on administration: for instance, we have to keep online records of what we've done each day and how long it took, so that the company can invoice clients. I also attend meetings about departmental issues and staffing, interview job applicants, give talks and presentations to clients and internal teams, and contribute to new business development.

What are the best things (and the worst) about your job?
The best things all revolve around the company culture – lots of the people I work with are informed, intelligent, challenging, relaxed and funny.

I suppose the worst aspects are due to the pressure of the new media industry, which means we work to very tight deadlines and don't always have time to take stock or review the way we approach problems.

Does the company generate its own social life after working hours?

Yes. One of its strengths is that people actually like each other and are always meeting socially – in the pub, on trips arranged by individuals, going to gigs, bowling etc.

Have you any advice for school leavers wishing to enter e-commerce?

Remember that somewhere in all the electronic customer relationship management programmes, systems software, user surveys, marketing targets, segmentation reports, jargon and abbreviations, there are real people trying to understand, acquire or achieve something.

Can you identify any qualities that make people more likely to succeed?

The main qualities are professional competence, high standards, clear thinking, perseverance, keeping a sense of perspective and a sense of humour.

What do you think the future holds for you/the industry?

I've never thought much about my future. I'll probably return to my own writing at some point.

The new media industry has now had its proving period and is here to stay – it's leaner, better understood, and commercially more influential than ever.

Commerce and corporate communications will inevitably continue to grow online, but I personally hope the web never becomes totally dominated by business, as sometimes seems to be the case.

CASE STUDY

Adrian Gill is Managing Director of V2 Internet, a small marketing, website development and e-commerce company based in Cheltenham, Gloucestershire. (UPDATE – Adrian has just overseen the merger of V2 Internet with Firehoop, another Cheltenham company with similar aims.)

How did you get your first job – and what was it?

My first job was in media for a huge Dutch company called VNU. I got the job by ringing their Human Resources department direct and getting the contact name responsible for the department I was interested in. I then called so many times they gave me an interview just to stop me calling!

As the job was sales focused I think they appreciated my persistence. Whatever the truth, I got the job. But, just to be on the safe side, at the same time I also went on to the job market through several recruitment agencies as a back-up.

What has helped you to progress?

Without question the biggest thing that has helped me progress is making and keeping contacts. Both internally when I was at VNU, and with clients, agencies and even competition, I made a point of getting to know as many people as possible and always listened to what they had to say. Listening is the most fundamental aspect to any business in my experience. Always take advice – you can choose to discard it once you've heard it but always take it – I've learned so much that way.

Can you summarise a typical working day?

My typical working day involves me juggling several job functions. First and foremost, as MD I have to ensure that the company is running smoothly. That means I have to get involved in everything from cash flow through to staff morale and personal issues.

Secondly I have to constantly look at revenue generation – whether it is getting new business or developing income from existing clients. This can only be done properly by getting out there and constantly putting yourself in front of the right people. I also have to make sure that all existing projects and current clients are on track and running smoothly. This is done day to day by account managers – it is for me to keep up to date with them to monitor the situation.

Finally, when we have got new projects I will need to sit down with the creative team, account management and developers to spec the project and put together various timelines and process flow charts. Presenting our plans to the client will also be a major part of my job.

What are the best things (and the worst) about your job?
The best thing is when you see a project you have been responsible for go live and generate income above and beyond client expectations. Also I find seeing the satisfaction that our employees get from their work very rewarding. Money has to feature somewhere! To work very hard, be successful and still be able to reap the benefits is clearly essential. Getting a healthy balance is vital – it's the old question, 'Do you work to live or live to work?'

I can't honestly think of the worst aspects – the long hours, perhaps.

Does the company generate its own social life after working hours?
Yes, I believe having a work hard culture in the company means you have to balance this with a play hard ethic as well. Having a team-based social life helps build team morale, especially across divisions internally, between account handling and creative teams for instance. In most companies there will invariably be politics. These arise from differences in opinion and values between account managers and developers, designers, sales teams and managers. But these political clashes don't have to fester. It's amazing how many bridges can be built over a drink!

Have you any advice for school leavers wishing to enter e-commerce?
Yes, try and get a decent work placement. Even if you have left school and all your friends are going for jobs to earn money, you'll find you need some experience to get ahead – if need be, get a job at an Internet company and offer your services free for a month. By getting into a company you will be able to see what you do and don't like within the industry and you will also be able to make useful contacts. The hardest part for a school leaver is getting experience.

Once you're in, if you find yourself just doing boring jobs (often the way of things early on), then do them with a smile and be seen to do them very well. Once you are confident and they know you are doing them with ease then you can feel more justified in asking for more responsibilty. Also, make a point of reading industry magazines and online newsletters to try and build up your knowledge of the industry. Have a look at big and small e-commerce sites and note down about them what you do and don't like and how, if at all, they could be made better.

Can you identify any qualities that make people more likely to succeed?

Good listeners always prosper, as I suggested earlier. Have a conscious knowledge gap, by which I mean you should know that there is so much you don't know and the only way you will find out is by asking questions and listening to the answers. Work hard and always, always work for the job you want – not the one you have.

So if you are a junior developer or an account executive, look at what is expected from the next step up and work that hard. It's not enough to do just enough. Don't be afraid to talk straight with your boss and tell her or him what you want. Thus, if you want to move forward and you are confident that you can do what is expected (and more) then ask. You might be pleasantly surprised with the result.

What do you think the future holds for you/the industry?

The Internet in general has had a bad press recently, with commentators everywhere saying it's in a slump. This may be true to an extent, but only due to the unrealistic promises and expectations that were floating around in the dotcom boom. The bottom line now is that the levels of revenue generated over the web are huge and many companies are succeeding.

The web is only another route to an intended market: it is not a miracle solution to any business. As the Internet becomes the norm, so more and more companies and sites will go over to e-commerce. The industry can only grow, as long as people remember to keep their feet on the floor.

For me personally, I see the future hopefully as growing the business into the leading Internet company in the south west and after that – who knows . . .

DID YOU KNOW?

Almost half a million UK businesses are currently trading online. Furthermore, one and a half million small to medium-sized UK companies have the capacity to do so as they are connected to the Internet, either via email or having their own websites.

SUCCESS STORIES

MARTHA LANE FOX (LASTMINUTE.COM)

After graduating from Oxford with a degree in Ancient and Modern History, Martha started her first job and met the future co-founder of lastminute.com Brent Hoberman. In October 1998 they launched lastminute.com, described as the dotcom site that 'uses the power of the Internet to match last-minute buyers with last-minute sellers'. It was an instant success. On Martha's 27th birthday, lastminute.com's flotation was announced, which subsequently valued the company at £732 million.

Like others, the company then suffered from the over-optimistic expectations that had caused it to be rated so highly and the consequent slump which hit the industry. However, because it offers a clearly defined service to a niche market, it has been able to survive the problems, albeit with a slightly lower valuation.

'I was very lucky because I got plenty of support and guidance from my family. They always encouraged me to think about doing different things or challenge myself. I'd been interested in travelling from quite a young age. I also had an incredibly cool history teacher who left a big impression on me.

My first job was at a very small start-up company – where I was engaged in doing strategy for media and telecoms companies and helping them think about new technologies. This was 1994, and it was here that I had the first inkling of setting up my own company.

Brent Hoberman had joined the business and whilst he and I were working together we often talked about setting up our own business. I decided to become a business partner with Brent before we even had a plan because I loved the idea.

It's very hard work. In a typical week I'm probably spending between 80–90 hours at work. You really need to have a great deal of energy, enthusiasm for customers, and tenacity in order to keep them. You also need to be able to work as part of a team – that's absolutely vital.

However, I can honestly say that every single day is different – that is one of the best things. Also I can dress for work as I want – I even came in my pyjamas once! But it normally depends on who I am meeting.

Other factors that are great about what I do are the people I work with and the people I get to meet. I do find that gives me a lot of mental stimulation.

I can definitely say that the least enjoyable part of my job is the long hours I have to work and that, in consequence, I scarcely have any friends left.'

PR ANATOMY OF AN E-COMMERCE LAUNCH

Sue Sillitoe helped to launch www.stylejunction.com as an e-commerce proposition in 2002 through her PR company, Dimes & Sillitoe. Here she gives an insight into why Style Junction, which provides a focal point for young artists and designers, decided to follow this route.

What was the stimulus for selling over the Internet?
The company felt there was huge potential to reach a wider number of customers if the concept and brand name could be established. The Internet offers a global shop window, which for a brand like Style Junction was important on two levels – to show its merchandise to all potential customers and to attract new designers from around the world who might want to market and sell original design items through the Style Junction site.

How did the founders set about getting funding?
All the funding came from private sources. This was obviously helpful because it is the most difficult hurdle for new e-commerce companies to overcome.

Has the venture proved successful?
In terms of raising brand awareness, it has so far been very successful. From a PR and marketing perspective, Style Junction has achieved plenty of press coverage, run a number of ad campaigns and generally got its name known. The business has made a number of sales via its site and continues to add new designers so that the range stays fresh.

How did it recruit its people?
All technical and administrative staff were recruited internally by its parent company, DCG. The current manager is Heloise Bontoux, who also came to Style Junction from the parent company. Dimes & Sillitoe was appointed via competitive tender from a number of PR agencies.

Is there any place for relatively inexperienced school leavers in the company?
Because we weren't involved in the original recruitment and selection processes we don't know.

What qualities do you think are necessary to do well in e-commerce?
For the company, deep pockets! Developing a consumer website takes time and money and you can't expect to survive on sales alone – at least not in the short term. It's also vital to build awareness for your site, by combining Internet marketing with conventional marketing – through press coverage, media campaigns, TV advertising, radio ads etc. For a person, the qualities must include perseverance, an open mind and a flair for taking calculated risks!

What, if anything, would you or the company change if you did it again?
From the PR point of view, I don't think we'd change much. We achieved good press coverage and it's still building. However I would still like to see Style Junction established as a portal for

the design community rather than just a retail site and I'm sure, in time, that will happen.

What types of product or service do you believe sell best through e-commerce?
Books, CDs etc are the easiest to sell – things that people don't really have to think about because they are inexpensive and familiar. Also, they are easy to transport and are not likely to break in transit. There is also a vast market for intangible services that are straightforward – buying car insurance, booking flights etc. Anything that increases speed and cuts down paperwork is a bonus.

THE TRAINER'S TALE

Annabel Greaves works as an Accredited Instructor for ExecuTrain. The company provides a range of IT training courses and instruction to corporate clients.

How did you get into the job?
Well, I certainly didn't join the company as a computer expert. ExecuTrain was looking for people who were interested in IT, had good communication skills, and would benefit from their training programme. It seems I fitted the bill.

Can you describe your training?
I underwent an intensive course through the company's Instructor Certification Programme. That was followed by four months of training, detailed study, and practical experience on a range of computer packages. I then felt confident in my ability to use the packages, and more important, felt ready and able to pass on those skills to others.

What and who do you teach?
I teach both beginner and advanced user courses dealing with a range of software including word processing, spreadsheets, and several different graphics packages such as PowerPoint, Freelance and Corel Draw.

Our clients are mainly individuals from large corporate companies. They range from secretaries to managers and directors. Some have never used a computer before, and others have some basic skills that they need to improve.

Can you run through a typical training session?

A typical class would consist of ten students. Before a session starts, I check all the equipment to make sure everything is working properly ready for a 9.30am start. At the beginning of a training session I introduce myself and try to put everyone at their ease. There are a number of strategies you can use to 'break the ice'. I usually get everyone to say a little bit about themselves.

The people in a session are from a range of backgrounds and all ages. In some sessions I'm teaching people who are twice my age, so it's important to be confident and demonstrate that you're on top of what you know.

It's also crucial to find out how much they already know, and you get used to being able to assess quickly what level the class is at. In what I would call a beginners' class I lead the students step by step through a set of exercises. I work at a computer at the front, facing the class, and everything I do is projected on a large screen behind me. As a session progresses I walk around the class and check to make sure that each individual understands what they're doing.

When a session is finished we don't just abandon the students to their fate. There's a support line that they can call if they're having any difficulty when they return to work. I collect these messages each day and get back to them to answer their queries.

At the end of each session I have some basic paperwork to do – evaluating each student – and they also evaluate my performance as an instructor. They fill out a score card that is sent to our head office, and at the end of the month an award is made to the trainer who scores most. I'm glad to say I've won a number of times!

Where do you teach?

Classes are held at our Exeter and Bristol branches, and often on the client's own premises. One day I could be working in Bristol and the next in London, so there's a good deal of travelling. Although we have a schedule of work laid out in advance sometimes there are changes at short notice and I have to drive to a different location. From time to time I also attend meetings with potential clients in support of our sales teams. I'm there to advise on training issues and answer other questions about training methods and so on.

Do you feel there are any particular qualities required?
This is a job that requires energy and commitment. You have to like working with people, be organised, punctual, well groomed, and ready with a smile, because you're always 'on stage'. There's no hiding place for the trainer.

What are your ambitions?
There are a number of career opportunities in the IT industry. I first want to gain more qualifications. Even though I'm an instructor, I'm also a student – there's always a lot to learn. The company allows us four days a month for study, so that we can keep up with developments as new packages come out or enhancements are made to existing ones. Eventually I'd possibly like to work for the company overseas. ExecuTrain has offices in Europe and America, so who knows, I may get to work in an exotic location one day.

DID YOU KNOW?
Three-quarters of all UK employees use computers at work and almost half (46%) do so to a moderately complex level.

CHAPTER 3

Training and apprenticeships

GROUP APPROACHES TO E-COMMERCE AND IT TRAINING

Here are details of a couple of useful group approaches to picking up information about working in IT and e-commerce.

GO FOR IT

Research shows that many people, particularly women, reject the idea of careers in IT because they have a negative image of it. This image is formed at around the age of 13 and, once formed, is difficult to change.

As a result there are currently IT skills shortages, which obviously have a negative effect on UK companies, and the country's overall competitiveness. Even during what might be described as a recession employers are finding it difficult, as mentioned earlier, to recruit the diverse workforce they need to represent their customer base.

In some areas you may find that local e-commerce and IT companies are devising workshops to be run at your school or college. If that opportunity crops up, take it. You will have a free, no-risk insight into how these businesses operate and it should confirm (or finish) your interest.

The scheme is known as Go For IT – you can learn more about it through Connexions (www.connexions.gov.uk). All the workshops have been devised to try to change the somewhat warped image that students (particularly young women) have of IT and e-commerce.

ITBEAT AWARDS

In fact, much of the marketing tends to be aimed at bringing women into the industry. As you will have gathered, young women are being put off at the moment by the 'techie' image that has grown up around e-commerce and IT.

The ITBeat Awards is a fansite competition for girls who may well have little or no interest in IT but will be tempted to enter because of the chance (if they reach the finals) to attend a glamorous celebrity event in central London where they can meet their idols, usually pop stars, film stars or TV personalities.

The aims of the project are to:

● invest IT with a touch of glamour;

● break down the first barrier to girls getting involved in IT – to show them that they can do it;

● get the 'Don't leave IT to the boys' message into the publications that girls and their parents and influencers read;

● make girls better informed about careers in IT.

The ITBeat Awards 2003 were held on 14 February (St Valentine's Day, in case you hadn't noticed) and the slumber party took place on 7 March.

INDIVIDUAL APPROACHES

However, the more usual method of acquiring the skills necessary to join an e-commerce or IT company is to make sure you get the training to enable you to join at any one of the levels listed below.

Don't take it to heart if you're still at school or just leaving, and you've been reading that many of the jobs require qualifications to degree level. Remember, everyone has had to start somewhere and there are now vocational or academic/vocational qualifications you can gain at every level to get your start in the e-commerce world.

OVERVIEW

- A great number of choices

- IT GNVQ (General National Vocational Qualification)/Vocational A-levels in IT

- A/AS level in Computing

- Vocational A-levels

- Highers (Scotland)

- HNC (Higher National Certificate)

- HND (Higher National Diploma)

- Foundation degree

- Vocational degree courses

- Postgraduate conversion courses

- Choosing your course.

A GREAT NUMBER OF CHOICES

There is a fantastic range of courses and qualifications for people of all ages looking to start a career in IT and for IT professionals and users wanting to improve or add to their existing skills: from post-16 academic and vocational qualifications, work-based training, through to vendor and professional qualifications.

This section should give you an idea (but in no way a comprehensive nor complete picture) of the type of courses and qualifications available and, to some extent, show how they relate to each other.

For a searchable database of courses in your area, go to www.learndirect.co.uk (for England and Wales – tel. 0800 100 900) or to www.learndirectscotland.com (for Scotland – tel. 0808 100 9000).

For those of you in England, the Qualifications and Curriculum Authority (QCA at www.qca.org.uk) is developing with its partner regulatory authorities in Wales (www.accac.org.uk) and Northern Ireland (www.ccea.org.uk) a coherent and easy to follow national framework of qualification (as shown in the table below) to guarantee quality and standards, meeting the full range of needs you will have at every level.

LEVEL OF QUALIFICATION	GENERAL	VOCATIONALLY RELATED	OCCUPATIONAL
5			Level 5 NVQ
4			Level 4 NVQ
3	A-level	Vocational A-level (Advanced GNVQ)	Level 3 NVQ
2	GCSE grade A*-C	Intermediate GNVQ	Level 2 NVQ
1	GCSE grade D-G	Foundation GNVQ	Level 1 NVQ
Entry level	Certificate of educational achievement		

You will find that QCA has also worked with its regulatory partner in Scotland (www.sqa.org.uk) to ensure that the National Vocational Qualifications and Scottish Vocational Qualifications give you the same levels of learning based on national occupational standards.

DID YOU KNOW?
During last year (2002) more than 100,000 students in England were completing their first year of GCSE Computing Studies. The equivalent figures for Scotland and Wales were 21,000 and 10,000 respectively. There are no numbers currently available for Northern Ireland.

IT GNVQ/VOCATIONAL A-LEVELS IN IT

The IT GNVQ is a general vocational qualification taught in schools, sixth form and FE colleges. It is designed to give you the broad foundation of skills and knowledge required for employment in the IT industry. You can take an IT GNVQ as a stand-alone course or in conjunction with other vocational or academic qualifications such as NVQs, GCSEs or A and AS levels. There are three levels of qualification:

- Foundation level entry requirements at age 16 – None;

- Intermediate level entry requirements at age 16 – GCSEs at grades D–G;

- Vocational A-level entry requirements at age 16 – 4 GCSEs at grades A–C.

A/AS LEVEL IN COMPUTING

Recent changes to the post-16 curriculum have made it easier for you to study a range of subjects and to combine traditional A-level study with vocational subjects. Key skills are now also an important part of A-level study and students can expect to gain qualifications in Communication, IT and Application of Number.

(See the Key skills section.) You will find you normally have to study for A/AS levels in sixth forms and FE colleges over two years:

YEAR 1
You take four or five subjects to AS (or Advanced Subsidiary level, as it is known in full) and gain a qualification for each subject you pass.

YEAR 2
In the second year you will normally carry on with two or three of your subjects (either those most useful or your best subjects) for full A-level qualifications.

JARGON BUSTER
Academic means studying for the sake of passing exams, although it may also help you find a job – vocational means studying to help you both find a job and be ultimately successful in your job.

VOCATIONAL A-LEVELS

Vocational A-levels have recently replaced Advanced GNVQ courses. You can take them by themselves or in combination with traditional A-levels. You're able to choose between:

- 3 unit – equivalent to an AS level;

- 6 unit – equivalent to an A-level;

- 12 unit – equivalent to 2 A-levels.

HIGHERS (SCOTLAND)

If you live in Scotland, the Scottish system also allows you to combine traditional academic and vocational study and there is a wide range of available subjects. They are called Highers and are available at five levels from Access to Advanced Higher. For further information, visit the SQA website at www.sqa.org.uk.

HIGHER NATIONAL CERTIFICATE (HNC)

What is a Higher National Certificate?
Basically it is a vocational qualification. You study at college but your experience of work from your job is also taken into account so it isn't just exam based.

The course is usually taken part time, perhaps taking one full day and a few evenings a week so that you can work and study at the same time.

HNCs have been available for quite a few years now and your employer may be willing to support you in some way, perhaps with some time out from work or some help with the fees. You can also find other ways of raising money for the course (see the Financial assistance section).

How long does it take?
Usually it takes two years, although many colleges offer different ways of studying for this qualification, so you may be able to do it more quickly, or take even longer, depending on the circumstances.

What subjects are there?
You'll find HNCs are available in a wide range of subjects, but if you are interested in a career in e-commerce and IT, the best ones for you are naturally HNCs specifically to do with IT and computing. There is quite a choice of these, so you need to check with a number of colleges to find out what they offer.

Where can I study?
In a wide variety of places – HNCs are provided by both colleges of further education and higher education, and by some universities.

What qualifications do I need to get on a course?
Usually one or two A-levels, a vocational A-level in IT or an NVQ Level 3 achievement and some work experience. If you count as one of the more mature applicants (in other words over 21) you may be able to get on to an HNC course with very little in the

way of formal qualifications, but you must have relevant
experience and show that you are prepared to do the work.

What can I do next?
Progression from an HNC to an HND or degree course is often
possible. Check this option with colleges that interest you.
You'll find that in some universities and colleges HNC/HND
qualifications are starting to be replaced by Foundation degrees.

HIGHER NATIONAL DIPLOMA (HND)

What is a Higher National Diploma?
Basically, it is a full-time version of the Higher National Certificate.
It is a vocational qualification, which emphasises practical
approaches to learning, including project and assignment work,
team and group work, and research into real business practice.

An HND is usually a full-time course. Many HNDs include work
placements of up to one term, and in some cases it may be
possible to have a complete year in industry gaining experience
that contributes to the achievement of the final qualification.

HNDs have been available for quite a few years now, and they are
widely accepted and understood by employers.

How long does it take?
Usually courses last two years, although many colleges offer
different ways of studying for this qualification, so you may be
able to do it more quickly, or take longer, depending on your
circumstances.

What subjects are there?
Once more, HNDs are available in a wide range of subjects, but if
you are interested in a career in e-commerce or IT, the best ones
for you are HNDs specifically to do with IT and computing. There
is quite a choice of these, so you need to check with a number of
colleges to find out what they offer.

Where can I study?
HNDs are provided by both colleges of further education and
higher education, and by some universities.

What qualifications do I need to get on a course?

Usually one or two A-levels, a vocational A-level in IT or an NVQ Level 3 achievement and some work experience. More mature applicants (people over 21) may be able to get on to an HND course with very little in the way of formal qualifications, but they must have relevant experience and show that they are able to do the work.

What can I do next?

Progression from an HND to a degree is often possible. Again, remember that in some universities and colleges, HNC/HND qualifications are starting to be replaced by Foundation degrees.

FOUNDATION DEGREES

Foundation degrees are new, employment-related higher education qualifications, designed to equip students with the skills that employers are looking for.

For general information on Foundation degrees for individuals, you should visit the DfES Foundation degree website at www.foundationdegree.org.uk. The site also features an interactive searchable database of some of the Foundation degree courses on offer by region and topic.

If you require further information, contact your local higher education provider to find out if they are offering this new qualification.

You can also call learndirect:

- for England and Wales – on 0800 100 900 or visit www.learndirect.co.uk

- for Scotland – on 0808 100 9000 or visit www.learndirectscotland.com.

VOCATIONAL DEGREE COURSES

About 10,000 students a year do decide to take an IT-related degree. Yet again, there is a bewildering variety of options and two courses can have very similar names with quite different content. In some universities the courses are highly practical, whereas others have a much more theoretical bias.

You will find that some courses span a broad area of study, whereas others such as Computer Games Design or Artificial Intelligence have a more specific focus. You can opt for a course that includes one or more industrial placements (highly recommended given what you are aiming for), and there are a variety of qualifications on offer including five-year programmes leading to M.Eng. degrees.

Entry qualifications vary between 6/8 UCAS points at A-level (the equivalent of two grades D and E) for the less sought-after courses and 30 points (three straight A grades) for popular courses at just a few universities. Some courses require Maths or a science at GCSE or A-level. Foundation courses are available in some universities for entrants who cannot initially meet all the usual entry criteria.

POSTGRADUATE CONVERSION COURSES

What are conversion courses?
As the name suggests, these year-long courses enable graduates who have not studied an IT degree to gain relevant knowledge and skills. They are available at many UK universities and generally lead to a Masters degree. Conversion courses are by no means all the same. Some are targeted at graduates from particular subject disciplines and aim to prepare their students for quite different areas of IT employment.

How do I set about finding out more?
A good initial source of information is the AGCAS survey 'Conversion Courses in Computer Science and IT', which is available on the Prospects website at www.prospects.ac.uk. It covers selection criteria, number of applications per place, typical jobs entered by graduating students and possible sources of finance.

CHOOSING YOUR COURSE

There is a great deal of information both on the web and in hard copy to help you make your choice. The Universities and Colleges Admissions Service (UCAS) website www.ucas.co.uk has details of all UK courses. The CRAC *Degree Course Guide* series, published by Trotman, includes one on Computer Science and Computing that has a lot of useful comparative information. The Trotman publishing site (www.careers-portal.co.uk) has a wealth of helpful detail. You might also find it useful to see what graduates do at the end of their degree courses; you can get summary information from the Higher Education Statistics Agency (HESA) site at www.hesa.ac.uk.

WORK-BASED TRAINING

NVQS AND SVQS

National Vocational Qualifications (NVQs) – in England and Wales – and Scottish Vocational Qualifications (SVQs) – in Scotland – are underpinned by occupational standards articulated and maintained by e-skills UK on behalf of employers.

NVQs/SVQs define what employees do in their jobs, based on practical skills demonstrated in the workplace. They help to validate and build on the technical but also personal and interpersonal skills that are vital to the sector.

There is no written test or examination with an occupational standard or vocational qualification. It is an assessment of the individual's ability to do his or her job competently to the required standard. So you are required to present evidence of competence taken from your everyday job. The assessment is performed by a qualified assessor, usually someone senior, who is experienced in the same area of work.

KEY SKILLS

Key skills are essential generic skills that you need for success in education, employment, lifelong learning and personal development. For example, they have been included as a component of the Modern Apprenticeship and Graduate Apprenticeship programmes that you will read about here.

They give candidates the chance to show their ability in the following areas:

- Communication

- Information Technology

- Application of number

- Working with others

- Improving own learning and performance.

Detailed information on Key skills can be found on the QCA website at www.qca.org.uk/ks.

MODERN APPRENTICESHIPS

The IT and Telecoms Modern Apprenticeships have been developed by industry through e-skills UK as a way of training young people to work effectively in their early careers.

Modern Apprentices are employed by an organisation and undertake both on and off-the-job training throughout their apprenticeship, possibly including attendance at college on a day-release basis.

Note that there are differences in the names according to which UK nation you are working in:

- England – Advanced/Foundation Modern Apprenticeships

- Wales – Modern Apprenticeships/National Traineeships

- Scotland – Modern Apprenticeships.

A Modern Apprenticeship consists of three strands that are interrelated and complementary, giving you an ongoing structure for training, development and progression:

1. For instance, gain an IT or Telecoms NVQ/SVQ:
   - at Level 3 for an Advanced Modern Apprenticeship (AMA)
   - at Level 2 for a Foundation Modern Apprenticeship (FMA).

2. Key skills such as those already mentioned:
   - Communication
   - Information Technology
   - Application of Number
   - Working with others
   - Improving own learning and performance.

3. Underpinning knowledge:
   - through the achievement of Vocational Related Qualifications (VRQs) and Technical Certificates (TCs).

You will find the e-skills website has general information on all types of Modern Apprenticeships that are related to IT and e-commerce. However, you should be aware that, as e-skills is an overall training standards body, their website cannot help you find a placement. But don't worry – many others can.

FINDING THAT PLACEMENT

There are several ways for you to look for a Modern Apprenticeship placement locally:

- Contact your local college and/or local training providers to find out if they offer the Modern Apprenticeships for IT users and for IT professionals.

- Check your local newspapers for adverts from employers or training providers offering Modern Apprenticeship places.

- If you live in England, contact your Local Learning and Skills Council (LLSC), which might have information on colleges, training providers and employers offering the Modern Apprenticeships in IT and IT-related subjects in your area. For contact details of your LLSC, go to www.lsc.gov.uk.

All Modern Apprenticeships will eventually include a Technical Certificate. In order to ensure the smooth implementation of these TCs a small number of 'pathfinder' frameworks have been identified to develop systems, processes and communication channels that will work effectively for you as these are brought into practice. These are:

- Accounting AMA

- Information Technology AMA

- Motor Industry FMA and AMA

- Sport, Recreation and Allied Industries FMA and AMA

Obviously it is the Information Technology AMA that is relevant here. Phased implementation of these programmes started in August 2002 and it is expected that Modern Apprenticeship frameworks will be available in all sectors from August 2003.

GRADUATE APPRENTICESHIPS

You should be aware that e-skills UK, in collaboration with employers and educators, has developed the e-skills Graduate Professional Development Award (GPDA), which represents the first stage of a structured professional development path for IT, e-commerce, IT related and telecoms professionals at entry level to the industry.

This is a development of what was in place beforehand. The e-skills GPDA was formerly known as the e-skills Graduate Apprenticeship (GA).

At the moment, e-skills GPDA students can specialise in either of the following:

1. An e-skills GPDA for IT
   In this module you will concentrate on two aspects of e-commerce and IT services:
   - Internet services delivery
   - Industrial management and industrial practice.

2. An e-skills GPDA for telecoms professionals
   For this programme you will be focusing on IT as it relates to the telecommunications industry.

If you are interested in either of these two programmes you should get in touch with your preferred GPDA centre – go to www.e-skills.com/cgi-bin/cms.pl/132 for contact details of where they're being run.

GRADUATES AND ON THE JOB TRAINING

If you're a graduate, as you've probably gathered, it's good news. Graduates are in strong demand across the range of e-commerce, IT and telecoms roles.

A primary objective is of course to help new graduate employees become effective and contribute to the business as quickly as possible. Most graduates, it is now recognised, whether from a technical background or not, will need practical training on the job.

DID YOU KNOW?
Apparently 56% of men in the UK have used the Internet, compared to 47% of women. Overall, 64% of people in the country have used computers.

RELEVANT TO THE WORKING WORLD

As mentioned earlier, the e-skills GPDA gives you a chance to forge a link with companies who might employ you at the same time as developing your skills. The programme has been developed and piloted with a range of employers, including small and medium-sized companies as well as major internationals such as Unisys, Hewlett-Packard and Compaq Computer Corporation.

These and other employers are forming agreements as needed with universities, higher education colleges or training providers to deliver underpinning knowledge elements of the programme.

Universities or colleges will form agreements in their turn with employers who can offer suitable workplace experience, which may be for short periods such as vacation work or for year-long placements. Check to see what's available in your area or further afield.

DEVISED TO SUIT YOU

The e-skills GPDA demands high standards, but its flexibility means it can be tailored to suit you and your individual employer.

You don't have to be a graduate either, despite the name. GPDAs are designed for a wide range of people:

● newly qualified graduates recently recruited to their first job;

● undergraduates part-way through their degree course who might be enrolled on to a GPDA programme while still at university;

● pupils/students at schools or sixth form colleges with A-levels or equivalent educational attainment including GNVQ, Baccalaureate;

● employees with A-levels or equivalent educational attainments or with a Foundation degree or other diploma;

● Modern Apprentices wishing to progress further.

So, a GPDA programme may start either during or following a degree course. Duration may vary: indeed it might be possible for an undergraduate to achieve a GPDA by the time of his/her graduation to a degree.

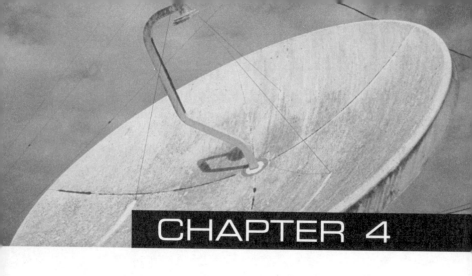

CHAPTER 4

Financial assistance

If you dig deep, there are various ways to finance your training and studies.

General information on financial help is available at www.learndirect.co.uk and www.learndirectscotland.com.

Information on financial aid in further education can also be found on the DfES website at www.dfes.gov.uk.

There are also several other sources of financial help:

● free and reduced rate courses

● help for people out of work

● Career Development Loans

● grants from employers

FREE AND REDUCED RATE COURSES

Free and reduced rate courses may vary in price, depending on length, content and provider.

All learndirect centres offer advice and free introductory courses to help you choose the right course for you.

The learndirect centre advisers will tell you the cost of the course you want and whether you can get financial help to pay for it.

You can call the learndirect helpline on 0800 100 900 or learndirect Scotland free helpline on 0808 100 9000.

HELP FOR PEOPLE OUT OF WORK

There is quite a lot of help available if you're out of work. Ask at the Jobcentre about New Deal and training schemes.

Local Learning Skills Councils also fund a wide range of courses for unemployed people. Contact your local LLSC (at www.lsc.gov.uk) or Jobcentre (at www.jobcentreplus.gov.uk) to see what's available in your area.

If you're planning to do some learning related to a job and you can't afford to pay for it, a Career Development Loan may be the answer.

CAREER DEVELOPMENT LOANS

These may help to get you started. You can apply to borrow between £300 and £8,000 to pay for:

● up to 80% of your course fees, as well as

● the full cost of books, materials and

● other expenses such as travel and childcare – and

● living expenses if it's a full-time course

- up to 100% of your course fees if you have been out of work for more than three months.

The Department for Education and Skills (DfES) pays the interest on the loan whilst you study. You don't need to pay back the loan until you've finished studying and are safely in a job. The DfES operates the scheme in partnership with four high street banks.

You can apply for loans of between £300 and £8,000 to pay for up to two years of training (or up to three years if the course includes work experience). The DfES pays the interest on the loan for the period of the training and for up to one month after. So, remember – as with all loans, the time for paying them back soon comes around.

If you want further information on Career Development Loans, you should go to www.lifelonglearning.co.uk/cdl or call freephone 0800 585 505.

GRANTS FROM EMPLOYERS

Your employer may be happy to fund your learning – especially if it relates to your work. Some help fund employees for any learning – they know they'll end up with more rounded, better motivated and interesting individuals and they also believe that there will be some loyalty payback from you.

Check whether your company has a personal development scheme or training programme – or whether they'll allow you paid time off for studying.

Larger organisations may also offer sponsorship. Read *Sponsorship for Students*, published by CRAC/Hobsons, for details of scholarships and bursaries.

MATURE PEOPLE WISHING TO ENTER IT OR E-COMMERCE

Just as it may sometimes seem as though the e-commerce world is slanted in favour of graduates, so it may also seem to older people that often this same world is deliberately ignoring them.

This is not the whole truth, and efforts are taking place to redress the gap. One such initiative for mature people is MaP>IT.

As defined for these purposes you are regarded as a mature person if you are over 40. Partly because of the shortfall in people coming through into the industry, a body called MaP>IT has been set up to help you acquire the necessary skills to cope with the challenges of IT and e-commerce.

Basically, MaP>IT is an anti-ageism initiative in the UK to help mature people fill IT skills gaps. It operates through a series of European Social Fund (ESF) financed UK regional initiatives, launched in 1999, to provide free IT training to mature employees of the UK's smaller and medium-sized enterprises (SMEs) and the self-employed.

Its objectives are to provide a sense of balance in e-commerce companies where the workforce is disproportionately young and age discrimination is rife, to increase the effectiveness of imminent legislation. MaP>IT also addresses the IT skills shortages that are restricting the development of many of the UK's SMEs.

There are currently two active ESF-financed projects in the London and eastern regions providing free IT training to the mature employees of SMEs and the self-employed. Further projects in other regions are due to come on stream later this year.

A wide range of these free computer courses, including European Computer Driving Licence (ECDL), CADCAM, PC Maintenance, Networking, eBusiness and Digital Entrepreneurship, is available, with most leading to a formal qualification.

Training can be taken as either classroom or Internet courses to fit in with business and other commitments and basic MaP>IT courses are also designed to build confidence in people who have not grown up with computers.

To qualify for MaP>IT training, you will as stated need to be over 40, and living or working in one of the designated MaP>IT areas, and either employed in a business with up to 250 employees or self-employed. MaP>IT is also unsurprisingly a government 'Age Positive' champion.

There are two UK areas providing this service at the moment:

- London: www.tru.ac.uk/mapit and

- East Anglia: www.acer.ac.uk/mapit.

CHAPTER 5

How to get the job you want

MAKE THE MOST OF YOURSELF

Here are a few suggestions on presenting yourself on paper to potential employers – how to write an eye-catching CV and a punchy covering letter.

Remember what the function of a CV is, namely to make you stand out from the crowd and get you an interview. So keep your CV short, no more than two pages, but provide employers with the sort of detail that will bring you to their notice.

If you haven't yet had many, or even any jobs, don't worry. The sort of detail that will be useful is to concentrate on your achievements and on the skills you've acquired – and make sure that those skills correspond with those that an e-commerce organisation will be looking for.

Tell them what your career ambitions are, by all means (checking of course to see that these are ones your target company might be able to fulfil).

Lay out your CV neatly and clearly, whether it is being sent by post or email. Check carefully to make sure everything reads well and is free from mistakes.

Compose your covering letter with great care so that it conveys your enthusiasm for joining the company without indulging in overselling.

For a full examination of how to present yourself on paper, try *Winning CVs for First-time Job Hunters* by Kathleen Houston (Trotman), which has excellent advice on every stage of the process.

TOP TIPS ON GETTING A JOB

There is such a wide range of job roles in e-commerce and IT that it is more than likely you can find a job that will suit you, whatever your background. Different jobs have very different skills requirements, so it is almost impossible to generalise. However most jobs, particularly the ones where you are working with customers, will need good interpersonal skills, teamworking and problem-solving ability.

IT jobs all have some technical content, ranging from the deep technical skills of a software developer through to roles that may need much less detailed knowledge – for example in some project management roles communication, organisation and the ability to gather together the people who do have technical knowledge may be more important than what you know yourself.

Some companies may be looking for experienced staff who have already been working in the industry, and ask for specific technical background or work experience. However many companies are also taking on people who are new to a career in IT.

You will discover a significant proportion are willing to take new recruits with little or no technical knowledge and offer training, provided you have other skills they value, such as interpersonal skills, and can demonstrate you are enthusiastic and capable of learning what you need to know.

How do you make them offer you work? Here are ten top tips that may help:

1. Do your research on your target company – in depth.

2. Prepare a relevant, customised CV.

3. Show you've got the energy, commitment and aptitude for e-commerce.

4. Gain any work experience you can.

5. Read everything about the industry you can get your hands on.

6. Apply for training programmes at your natural level (eg Modern Apprenticeships).

7. Snap up any free courses.

8. Develop other related key skills.

9. Be ready to do anything to gain a start.

10. Take all the luck you can find (but remember the harder you work, the luckier you get).

DID YOU KNOW?
Lack of basic computer literacy accounts for 30% of all the skills gaps reported in the UK. Why not make sure that won't apply to you?

If you are new to the industry, and want to increase your chances of getting a good job, think about how you can show that you are enthusiastic and capable of learning. An excellent way to demonstrate this is by getting work experience in something connected to IT.

You could also consider taking an extra course or qualification in an IT or business-related subject. And don't forget the importance of developing and demonstrating those other key skills, such as communications and problem solving.

Whatever your background it is always worth researching potential employers' interests carefully – you'll save time by applying to those who are really likely to be interested in you. Knowing as much as you can about their business will help as well.

Most employers, as you will discover, value key skills, such as communications, teamwork and problem solving just as much, if not more than technical skills. So you should definitely try to cultivate them.

If you are at university, the following documents will be of special interest (but they are useful to everyone as a general guide of what to aim for):

- The student booklet 'Have You Got What IT Takes?' concentrates on six employability skills, with examples of their use and ideas about how students can demonstrate them. Go to www.e-skills.com/pdfs/hygwit-students.pdf.

- The 'Skills Awareness Student Workbook' helps students assess their employability skills through a question-and-answer approach, and provides short exercises for each skill. It also includes active links to a variety of websites with further information. You can find this at www.e-skillsnto.org.uk/gemini/ – it is also part of the 'Have You Got What IT Takes?' series.

Many recruiters use psychometric tests as part of their selection process, particularly at graduate level. Many of the tests are particularly relevant if you are seeking a technical position but have no technical experience, as they can help employers to assess your potential for acquiring new skills.

The websites mentioned below have examples of tests, which you can try out. Your careers adviser can probably suggest which are most relevant. Most of the sample tests are aimed at graduate level. Don't be put off if you find some of them difficult since employers do not normally use a single test in isolation and, in any case, test results are just part of the selection process. Your interest, suitability and motivation matter too (not to mention all the many other factors that contribute towards selection decisions).

If you're not a graduate or studying to be one, you should also consider investigating these. If nothing else, it shows you what you might come up against.

Examples of tests:

- Saville & Holdsworth, the godfathers of psychometric testing in the UK, have examples of verbal, numerical and diagrammatic reasoning tests at www.shldirect.com.

- Sussex University Career Development Unit's site includes tips on taking tests, test examples and a list of other web resources. Go to www.sussex.ac.uk/Units/CDU/psycho.html.

- The Morrisby Organisation offers an emotional intelligence test at www.morrisby.com and links to other test sites, together with a test takers' guide.

- ASE offers a variety of practice tests at www.ase-solutions.co.uk.

- Psychometrics Inc. is a site geared primarily to recruiters choosing tests for potential programmers, computer operators etc. Whilst there are no actual practice tests, the general information about the tests is useful. Go to www.psy-test.com/TestIndex.html and for the UK www.psychometrics-uk.com.

If you want to apply for jobs that need you to have technical skills before you start, then a good source of what's in and what's not is the regular *Computer Weekly* survey at www.ComputerWeekly.com and similar surveys from *Computing* at www.vnunet.com. But don't just leap at what's currently fashionable – remember that things move very fast in the industry.

If you want to start a training course try to establish local employer interest in the qualification and get some practical work experience to back it up. If you are already studying and your programme doesn't include all the top skills, don't worry too much. For many employers evidence of your ability to learn one programming language is sufficient to convince them that you can quickly pick up parallel ones. Work experience and self-directed learning can also broaden your knowledge.

TRANSFERRING YOUR SKILLS

First of all, this is not an irreversible decision, and entering an e-commerce or IT job cannot ruin your life, even if you find you don't immediately enjoy the work. IT skills are so valuable in most jobs today that even if you found you wanted to change course you would find that what you have learned is of interest to a whole range of different employers.

Secondly, there is such a wide range of jobs that, unless you actively hate computers (in which case you're unlikely to be reading this), it is likely you can find an area where you could be happy. What you need to do is get clear in your own mind what it is about any job that would make you enjoy it. What skills do you enjoy using?

In many respects IT careers are no different from many others; you have to use a mixture of technical, logical, creative, organisational, team-building, problem-solving and communication skills. The trick is to figure out what you enjoy most, and then match your particular interests to the blend of skills required in a specific type of job. Reading descriptions of typical jobs, and learning as much as you can from other sources about what different roles entail, will help you decide what will suit you best.

There are many practical steps you can take to work this out. Being clear in your own mind will also help you to convince recruiters that you mean business. Try any of the following:

1. Talk to a careers adviser who can help you clarify what you want out of a job and how likely particular occupations are to meet your needs. Careers advisers can usually also offer questionnaires to help you decide what might suit your personality and interests.

2. As an alternative, use self-assessment questionnaires such as:

- Prospects Planner enables students in higher education to identify jobs that suit their skills, interests and personal values. For more information, see www.prospects.ac.uk and go to 'Where do I start?'
- Keirsey questionnaire at www.keirsey.com is a self-assessment questionnaire helping you to identify personality factors that can influence career choices and suitable work environments.
- The Morrisby Organisation gives some clues about searching the web and provides links to a range of interactive questionnaires, quizzes and tests at www.morrisby.com.

3. Network. Talk to people who already work in the industry. At careers fairs you can usually talk to fairly new entrants as well as more experienced staff and recruiters. For students in higher education, employer presentations offer the same opportunity. Go to as many as you can. You should also use your own contacts – somebody you know must work in IT or know someone who does.

4. Get as much work experience as possible. Careers staff can advise on how to go about it. Some useful sites include:

For school/college students
- www.vini.org.uk
  This site has post-A-level opportunities for a Year in Industry put together by the Royal Academy for Engineering (but includes all types of companies, not just engineering organisations).

For university students
- www.prospects.ac.uk
  Includes Focus on Work Experience, dates of work experience fairs and a database of opportunities.
- www.ncwe.com
  The site of the National Centre for Work Experience – highly useful.

- www.step.org.uk
  Information on eight-week summer placements, carrying out projects to help small businesses and much more.
- www.experienceworks.ncl.ac.uk
  Go to the students' page for work experience opportunities and how to get them.

CHAPTER 6

What resources do you need to support you?

Here's a list of some helpful websites that can help you get your first piece of work experience or full-time job in e-commerce and IT.

CAREERS

www.careers-portal.co.uk
A well-established award-winning careers information site from Trotman publishing.

www.careers-gateway.co.uk
A general site for careers and job search information.

www.careersoft.co.uk
This site is mainly for secondary school students and is linked to the previous site.

www.hobsons.co.uk
Careers information for everyone from school leavers through to
postgraduates.

www.prospects.ac.uk
A comprehensive careers site for students in higher education.

www.insidecareers.co.uk/it
A useful source of career advice with details of the latest
graduate vacancies.

www.doctorjob.com
An information site for what they call 'graduate careers with
attitude'.

NON-GRADUATES

The British Computer Society website at www1.bcs.org.uk/ has a
useful job-hunting section (under 'Advice').

The following sources are also helpful if you are seeking a first
job in the industry.

WITH GCSE, A-LEVEL OR EQUIVALENT QUALIFICATIONS

Your local careers service company – you can find your local
contact at www.careers-uk.com.

Jobcentres – electronic terminals now give access to vacancies all
over the country. For information on all these you can go to
www.jobcentreplus.gov.uk.

Alternatively, contact your Local Learning and Skills Council (for
England) – you can find information at www.lsc.gov.uk.

If you live in Wales, you need the Council for Education and
Training Wales – you can find them online at www.cetw.org.uk.

Or go to your Local Enterprise Company (for Scotland) – either
through Highlands and Islands Enterprise (at www.hie.co.uk) or
Scottish Enterprise (at www.scottish-enterprise.com).

For Northern Ireland, you need the Training and Employment Agency at www.tea-ni.org.uk.

Local newspapers can be a good source of job advertisements, especially if you're starting your career. For links to local papers, you should go to www.thepaperboy.com.

Recruitment consultancies – The Recruitment and Employment Federation website has a database searchable by job type and location at www.rec.uk.com.

WITH A DEGREE (IT OR NON-IT) OR A POSTGRADUATE QUALIFICATION

Your university careers service – www.prospects.ac.uk has links to all UK universities.

Directories of graduate IT career opportunities such as:

● Prospects Focus on IT – www.prospects.ac.uk

● Hobsons' *Guide to Careers in IT & Communications* – www.hobsons.com

● Inside Careers Information Technology – www.insidecareers.co.uk

● Target IT – www.gti.co.uk

You should check the national job vacancy bulletins – Prospects Today (if you have completed your course or are soon to do so) and Prospects Finalist (for current students) – both online at www.prospects.ac.uk.

You can always explore any leads from your academic department if you are studying for an IT-related degree.

Careers and IT careers fairs – the Prospects website lists dates and locations at www.prospects.ac.uk

TRADE PRESS

Computer Weekly at www.ComputerWeekly.com (also available in print format).

Computing at www.vnunet.com, which also gives you access to other IT-related journals (and again, is also available in print format).

DID YOU KNOW?
62% of all people working in the UK say that IT and e-commerce skills will be essential to progress in their jobs, or to help them find other jobs. 53% said that basic skills would be vital in the short term (two to three years) and 47% felt that acquiring more advanced skills would be necessary – even in the short term.
